On Life
(Things I Should Have Told You)

Kim Nelson

BookLocker
Saint Petersburg, Florida

DISCLAIMER

This book details the author's personal experiences with and opinions about various aspects of managing one's lifestyle. The author is not a licensed a licensed medical, legal, financial or accounting professional.

The author and publisher are providing this book and its contents on an "as is" basis and make no representations or warranties of any kind with respect to this book or its contents. The author and publisher disclaim all such representations and warranties, including for example warranties of merchantability and advice for a particular purpose. In addition, the author and publisher do not represent or warrant that the information accessible via this book is accurate, complete or current.

Any statements made about products and services have not been evaluated by the U.S. government. Please consult with your own legal, accounting, medical, or other licensed professional regarding the suggestions and recommendations made in this book.

Except as specifically stated in this book, neither the author or publisher, nor any authors, contributors, or other representatives will be liable for damages arising out of or in connection with the use of this book. This is a comprehensive limitation of liability that applies to all damages of any kind, including (without limitation) compensatory; direct, indirect or consequential damages; loss of data, income or profit; loss of or damage to property and claims of third parties.

You understand that this book is not intended as a substitute for consultation with a licensed medical, legal or accounting professional. Before you begin any change your lifestyle in any way, you will consult a licensed professional to ensure that you are doing what's best for your situation.

This book provides content related to lifestyle topics. As such, use of this book implies your acceptance of this disclaimer.

To my sweet girls, whom I will always love as only a mother can love a daughter.

–Mom

A mother's love for her child is like nothing else in the world. It knows no law, no pity. It dares all things and crushes down remorselessly all that stands in its path.

–Agatha Christie

Contents

INTRODUCTION

What lies behind you and what lies in front of you, pales in comparison to what lies inside of you.

—Ralph Waldo Emerson

It is suddenly over. These glorious eighteen years we've spent together (well, almost nineteen, if you count the nine months you spent inside of me). Living together in one house, tucked within the intimate cocoon of family, has been an amazing experience. Stumbling down for breakfast each morning, gathering at the front door waiting for your school bus before you could drive, doing puzzles, having dance parties, cuddling up on the couch to watch a movie, playing cards, making cookies, putting on facial masks, sitting down for dinner—all the simple everyday activities that people who live in the same house do together—will now be neatly folded away into a box labeled "your childhood." Knowing we will see you each morning and afternoon or evening, however briefly, is something we've come to take for granted. We will miss you terribly. Every single day.

Raising you reasonably well has been your father's and my greatest aspiration in life. You are all we hoped you would be—and more. Getting to know you from the first days we held you in our arms until now, and seeing you step out and away from us, has brought us immense joy. We will serve as your memory keepers for the rest of your life (even for those you'd rather forget). We will hold your childhood close and dear; it will be forever fresh in our minds—your likes and dislikes, your ups and downs, your happy moments and sad ones. We have loved learning who you are and watching you change, grow, and mature. You are kind, smart, beautiful, hardworking, and capable. You are ready to create your future. I think.

I find myself wondering if we have adequately prepared you for all that you will encounter out in that wild and woolly world—if I have told you everything I wanted you to know. There have been things I wanted to say but knew would be met with a groan and eye roll and so bit my tongue. Now I am wishing I had said them anyway, so at least you would know how I feel about so many things that matter to me—for later, when they will matter to you. And so, I decided to write them down.

As I began to think of all the things I wanted to say to you but did not, it occurred to me that my advice might not even be valid. I got to discover my own truths, so why shouldn't I step aside and let you do the same? Who am I to offer advice, after all? I certainly haven't gotten it all right. And who wants to hear someone else pontificate about what they believe is important? The truth is, while I haven't gotten it all right, I have gotten some things right. I have been happy, healthy, and prosperous. I have loved deeply and been loved by others. I have lived a good life (in my own judgement, anyway).

And as I have moved through this world, I've come to see that none of it was a given. Life is a series of choices, and as with all journeys, it's not a bad idea to have a general framework to help you think about getting from point A to point B. By the way, there is nothing new you will read in this book that you haven't picked up from living with your father and I, from school, from sports, from going to church. You have the bits and pieces of this framework inside of you. This book is simply my attempt to summarize it all in one place.

In my life, I have tried hard to create positive change, to make things better when they were not right, and to help others. And more and more, I am realizing that these are the things that have mattered most. I want you to wake up in your late 50s and feel like you have lived a life of worth and that you have become the person you always wanted to be. I want you to feel that the world is an exciting and amazing place, filled with possibilities that you can shape to benefit yourself and others.

And so, I want to share what I know, what I have learned in these fifty-seven years, the "hard-fought wisdom I have earned," and you can take the best and leave the rest. Your truths may be different. But at least you will have mine. They are the most precious gift I can give you.

You may never read all of the reflections in this book. You may read two or three of them. You may read them and then forget or ignore them, or you may simply disagree with them. But I thought it would be better for you to have them than not, and I leave it to you to do with them what you will.

I can't wait to watch your life unfold. You father and I will always be here for you, cheering on your successes, commiserating with your failures (and you will have plenty—everybody does), urging you to pursue your dreams, and encouraging you to seize the opportunities available to you (or create new ones). But most of all, we will always be here to just love you as you are, for who you are.

ON FAMILY

You don't choose your family. They are God's gift to you, as you are to them.

—Desmond Tutu

I will start with family, because I have come to believe it is the most important source of happiness in life. Your family has known you since your birth and will be uniquely attached to you forever. The trick with family is that it does need care and feeding. Finding time to call or send a text is important. You may only see some family members once a year or once every five years, but they are still family and you should work to stay in touch. They will bear witness to your life.

I hope you are lucky enough to fall in love, marry, and have children of your own. Some people think of kids as a burden, an obstacle to achieving their hopes and dreams, and a constraint on their own pleasures and desires. They see only the 4 a.m. feedings, dirty diapers, and endless messy chaos associated with children, particularly when very young.

They are not wrong. Those things are real. Raising kids is incredibly challenging and often stressful. But being a parent is also the most fulfilling, exciting, transformational event that can happen in a person's life. It changes you forever, in the ways that matter most. Kids teach us to be selfless and to care for others at the most basic, fundamental level. I've often reflected that there is nothing I have ever done in my professional career that comes close to the profound sense of joy, purpose, and accomplishment I have found as a mother.

Keep track of your sister, your grandparents, cousins, aunts, and uncles as best you can as your life unfolds. Establish independent relationships with them. Call them and go to dinner when you are in a town where family lives. You are blessed to be born into a loving, healthy, vibrant, extended family, and you have a responsibility to share them with your kids.

Notice I didn't mention Dad and me. You don't have to worry about keeping track of us—we will keep track of you!

ON HEALTH

A healthy man has many wishes; a sick man has but one.

—Indian proverb

Your health is, quite simply, all you really have. The good news is that maintaining it is largely in your own hands. For the most part, you control your destiny and can shape it by the choices you make to take care of the marvelous gift of your body. Your body is perfect in its ability to adapt, heal, stretch, grow, endure, and support your life goals.

I know you understand the importance of eating right and getting plenty of exercise. You see how great your grandmother looks and what she is able to do—pretty much anything I can do, and she is eighty-two years old! How many eighty-two-year-olds walk three miles a day? This is the return you get on a lifetime of investing in your health.

There is no big secret to health. Eat lots of fruits and vegetables, not a lot of meat or sugary foods, avoid junk food, and exercise for an hour every day. Drink a lot of water. Don't smoke and don't drink a lot of alcohol or do drugs. Get a lot of sleep. If you can generally live within these guidelines, you will likely enjoy lifelong health. Easy-peasy.

I want you to know that health is not just about not getting sick; it's about feeling great every day. It's about having the energy to do what interests you. It's also not just about your body. Mental health is just as important.

Feeling reasonably good about yourself is at the core of mental health. Understanding that you are capable, lovable, and powerful is a good place to start. Meditation (which I never mastered), prayer (my version of meditation), and taking time to just be quiet and relax are all important to your mental health. Also, it's helpful to surround yourself with people who bring you energy versus deplete it. I recommend spending as little time as possible with people who create stress in your life—personal or professional. You know who I mean, people who wrap drama around themselves like a cloak. Do not tolerate people who say mean things to you, berate you, or cause you to feel "less than." Life is too short. Surrounding yourself with positive people who like you for who you are and support your goals will go a long way in ensuring your mental health. The children's book author, Dr. Seuss, got it right when he said, "Be who you are and say what you feel, because those who mind don't matter and those who matter don't mind."

Lastly, spiritual health is important too. I know you are not a religious person and your own spiritual beliefs are still evolving. I want you to know how deeply I respect that. It means you are thinking for yourself. By the way, when I was nineteen, I was just as skeptical as you are. But I also want you to be aware that having a serious spiritual life—whatever that looks like for you—is important. The faith tradition that makes the most sense to you is less important than having an objective way of understanding morality and a clear vision of how we ought to treat one another during our brief time here on earth.

Having beliefs about life and death are helpful. When you have children, in particular, this takes on even greater significance. You may find you want to provide them with a religious framework and let them make their own choices from a place of knowledge versus ignorance when they are able, as you have had the freedom to do.

I pray that you continue to intentionally explore what it is you believe, because what you believe will help you determine who you want to be and how you want to move through the world and this life. I would be lying if I didn't tell you that I hope one day you find your way to a higher power. Pay attention to the beliefs of people you respect. That helped me find my way. Listen. Ask for help. Keep an open mind. See what happens. You are loved, and there is most definitely a source of that love. Find it.

ON COURAGE

I learned that courage was not the absence of fear, but the triumph over it. The brave man is not he who does not feel afraid, but he who conquers that fear.

—Nelson Mandela

The world is a wonderful place but also a scary and an intimidating one. We are engineered to be attuned to danger—and we see it everywhere. This state of high alert is probably what kept us alive as a species thousands of years ago. As Thomas Hobbes said, for much of human civilization, life has been "solitary, poor, nasty, brutish, and short." There have always been so very many ways to die and so much to be afraid of. In our modern world, however, what many of us are most afraid of is nothing more than experiencing failure or suffering embarrassment. These are universal fears. It's helpful and smart to remember that you are not in any way unique if you have these fears or anxieties. *We all have them.* The difference is in *how* we handle them.

Fear can be debilitating and incapacitating. Courage is the ability to move through and past fear and take action. This is true in all arenas. It takes practice to conquer fear, but it is a worthwhile endeavor. Push yourself whenever you can to move toward what scares you in life. All growth happens in the margins, when we are interfacing with the unknown. Think of a child learning to walk. They are too young to fear falling. If they did, they would never learn to walk, for they will fall many, many times—and so will you.

When you and your sister were younger, you were gymnasts. One of the things I love about gymnastics is the routinization of failure. The entire sport is *all about* failure—falling off beams and bars, missing vaults, missing tumbling sequences. Even the very best gymnasts routinely fail—publicly—at meets. I can't imagine how much courage it takes to do a double back handspring on a four-inch wooden beam four feet off the floor. When learning a new skill, gymnasts fail again and again and again, until they master it. How wonderful! I wanted you and your sister to learn that failure is *a part* of learning. I once heard a speaker at a sales meeting say she thinks about the word fail as an acrostic for her "first attempt in learning." This kind of mindset is invaluable.

Of course, the situations you will fear as a young adult will be less about your physical well-being and more about saying or doing something embarrassing. You may be afraid to speak up in class to share your perspective if it seems at variance with those around you. You may be worried about how to act or what to say in a social setting that is unfamiliar. You may feel that others around you are smarter, prettier, or otherwise superior to you, and you may find that intimidating and fear embarrassing yourself. And so, you may silence or edit yourself—or avoid settings where you have to risk saying or doing the wrong thing. This would be a mistake and a terrible habit to develop.

There is also the matter of having courage to speak out when something is wrong or doesn't make sense. Or having the courage to speak on behalf of someone who is being wronged when they can't find their own voice. Sometimes something as simple as speaking the truth—especially to those in authority—requires courage. We call this speaking truth to power. You will grow stronger each time you overcome your fears and say and do what you know to be right.

The problem is that if you become too anxious to avoid failure, you will do only the things you know how to do and confine yourself to situations in which you feel comfortable. Beware of this temptation. It is extremely limiting. It will prevent you from trying new things that will be amazing for your personal development and growth. Get comfortable with discomfort. Hold yourself in the space of discomfort so you learn how to conquer it. All great endeavors in life require risk-taking, and inherent in risk-taking is the possibility, even likelihood, of failure. Embrace it.

It gets easier, by the way. The fear never goes away, but your confidence in navigating it strengthens. Like most things in life, if you practice, you get better. Each situation you overcome builds confidence, and you'll have more courage available the next time you find yourself in a challenging situation. You just have to stick with it.

ON LOVE

When it comes to matters of the heart, there ain't a thing a fool won't get used to.
                                    —Michael McDonald

One of the greatest mysteries of life is why we love whom we love. And one of life's greatest wonders is that there is actually someone out there for each of us, able to love us completely, with wild abandon. In fact, there are many people out there just waiting to love us, because each of us is unequivocally lovable, warts and all. I think this is why love is the most powerful force on earth.

It reflects acceptance, which every human being craves. It enables sacrifice. It makes us selfless and calls us to be our best selves, and it brings us joy.

You will likely fancy yourself "in love" at least a few times in your life (and perhaps already have). All romantic love starts with attraction, which blooms into infatuation, followed by obsession. Infatuation is an all-consuming maelstrom that distracts you from pretty much everything else important going on in your life. You are thinking of the object of your desire constantly. Wondering what they are doing, what they are wearing, when you will see them again, and if they are thinking of you. It is such an intense emotion, and you feel so "caught up" in it while it's going on, it almost feels like you are drugged in those heady first days, weeks, and months.

Here is the problem. Like most drugs, the high doesn't last. If it's not reciprocal, it's a nightmare. You think it's love, they think its sex—an age-old dynamic that always ends badly. If you are the object of someone else's unreciprocated devotion, it's flattering for your self-esteem for a minute, but gets annoying pretty quickly.

If it's mutual, it's amazing! For a while, anyway. Eventually the intensity of emotion subsides, and one or both of you wake up one day and realize this person you thought was perfect actually has flaws. You gradually become less interested in spending every waking moment together. In mature love, you process the flaws, but decide the things that are amazing about the person outweigh the things you don't care for.

If this is not the case, you begin to feel trapped in the relationship and start looking for the exit—or they do. If you are the person dumped, it rips your world apart. I sound dramatic, but trust me, these words will be ringing in your ears one day (and maybe you have already experienced this wrenching pain). Losing love is absolutely soul-crushing. The good news is that the pain subsides over time, and you move on to new experiences, new loves. The first time is the worst.

The bad news is that you have to keep at it, if you ever hope to find "the one." You have to keep taking the risk, taking that plunge, which is all the worse because after the first time, you *know* how bad it can be if you fall hard, and things don't work out.

But then, one day, things do work out. The infatuation fades but is replaced by a deep, passionate connection and enduring respect. These feelings strengthen the more you get to know one another. The more time you spend together, the more "right" the relationship feels. You start to wonder if this might be the right person, the right time in your life. You start thinking, could he or she be "the one"? You start wondering what kind of parent they would be, what your children would look like. You start wanting the people you care about in your life to meet your loved one. Your friends. Your sister. You will know you are really serious if you want your father and me to meet them.

It will be an amazing time in your life.

ON DRUGS AND ALCOHOL

Drugs are a waste of time. They destroy your memory and your self-respect and everything that goes along with your self-esteem.

—Kurt Cobain

Y ou will likely experiment with drugs and alcohol as you make your way through the next four years. I know we have talked about this ad nauseam, but I just want to put my thoughts down on paper, because the situations you will be facing as you step out of your cocoon will be more intense and challenging than anything you have experienced in high school.

You will have a tremendous desire to fit in, to be cool, to make friends, to do what is done "in college." This will all take place just as you are finding your footing and defining who you are; deciding what you want and don't want to do. It is a tricky time in your life—and it can go horribly wrong, very quickly. I have seen this firsthand and have heard stories from friends a few years along on this journey with their kids.

For some reason, the stakes seem higher than when I was in school. You can really be hurt badly out there. Most bad things that happen do so in the wee hours when women are drunk or high and don't have their wits about them. Ironically, when you are doing drugs or drinking, part of the effect of the substance is to impart a sense of confidence and invulnerability. You will think to yourself, *I've got this*, precisely when you most definitely do not. You are at your least competent when you are high.

Here is the deal. You don't want to be "that girl." You know which girl. Her eyes are glazed over, she's slurring her words, and she looks like she might hurl any moment, or maybe she already did but is so wasted she doesn't even realize it. There are guys around her, not girlfriends, because girlfriends would not allow her to be in this state in public. Not real friends. They would gently ease her out of there and get her safely to her dorm room where she could sleep it off.

But this girl we are talking about is vulnerable because she is impaired. Most young men are not going to take advantage of this girl. But some will. And the very small minority of young men around who are flat-out predators definitely will. If you doubt me, watch the documentary, *The Hunting Ground*. It should be required viewing for every high school senior heading to college—male and female.

The guys trailing this girl will be looking to find some way to get her alone. Afterward, she may make it back home that night, or perhaps it will be the next morning. She will be mortified. She will be humiliated. She won't want to report what happened to anyone. Or she may not remember, which is a kind of mercy and penance at the same time, because others will, and she won't know what they remember about her.

Do not be that girl.

There will be other guys at that party who will be embarrassed for "that girl." They may laugh at her antics because they are not quite sure how to handle the situation. Even if they are laughing, they may be uncomfortable—but not uncomfortable enough to intervene. It takes a lot of courage to intervene. These young men are as susceptible to male peer pressure as anyone. They may even move closer to watch the spectacle.

The person you want to watch for is the young man of worth. This is the guy who has the courage and self-confidence to gently extract this girl from the predicament she is in. He will use humor with the other guys and draw on his own personal credibility. He will find a way to get her out of there, often with the assistance of a woman, and get her safely to her dorm. By the way, this is a rare person. Really special. This is the kind of guy you want to pay attention to.

Remember, once you start drinking or drugging, you lose your judgment and therefore your ability to moderate. Things can get out of hand quickly. I know you have seen this already in high school.

I do understand that you will want to experience all that college life has to offer and to experiment. You are an adult, and why should I try to stop you? I have had the privilege of forming my own beliefs based on my own experiences. Why shouldn't you? I don't want to stop you from experimenting. I couldn't if I wanted to, anyway. I just want you to be smart and safe. Be careful.

Make sure you always have one or two women (or men) around you whom you trust to make smart decisions for you if you can't. Think about your strategies for the evening in advance. What about sipping one drink all night? This way, you avoid people continually bringing drinks to you—and they will. Think about the language you will use. "I'm good," or "I just got this drink," or "I've got to use the bathroom." Be prepared to witness behavior that will raise your eyebrows and be ready to stand confidently in the space of who you want to be.

It's good to have your wits about you in social settings. I never liked being out of control, because I like to know what's going on. I don't like slurring my words. I don't like falling down or knocking things over or bumping into people. I can better assess others if I am not impaired myself. I want to have fun but not be unable to think clearly. Or worse, have to leave because I feel sick.

There is another risk to be wary of as you think about drugs and alcohol: addiction. You are smart enough to know that addiction is a real thing. No one starts out thinking, *I want to be an addict. I want this substance to take over my life and control my plan for each day and dominate my thoughts.* And yet, many people end up there, and not a few are first exposed in college. I know you have seen the vaping phenomenon play out in high school and have friends who became addicted, so you know this is real. The same thing can happen with drugs and alcohol. Trust me. If it were not true, there would be no rehabilitation clinics.

Go forth, enjoy the parties, have fun. But be safe, be smart, and be careful.

ON SOCIAL JUSTICE

In this world, I won't count for much, unless I stand for you.

—Michael McDonald

You can't live a perfect day without doing something for someone who will never be able to repay you.

—Coach John Wooden

You have been raised with great privilege and great opportunity. It is not fair that every child does not have the benefit of growing up in a loving home, where there is a quiet place to do homework. Or of going to a great school, competing in sports, or otherwise developing their body, mind, and spirit. In many ways, it is priceless to get to fully be a child, absorbed in the concerns of children and unconcerned with adult matters or responsibilities.

There are alternate realities, lived by millions of children all over this country and world. I wish I could say hundreds, or hundreds of thousands, but it is, literally, millions. I start with children, because while adults suffer as well, children are the most vulnerable. They are entirely at the mercy of the adults around them. They have no control over their environment and cannot fight back or walk away. They were born utterly pure and innocent and have done nothing wrong. They don't deserve the childhood that fate has dealt them.

The most heinous criminals were once adorable, innocent infants. They were all three years old, then five, and then eight or eleven, but when they turned thirteen, and then sixteen, the consequences of their upbringing begin to harden. And then, suddenly, at eighteen, they are adults, and no one is thinking about the childhood that produced the dangerous person moving through society.

No one remembers that this adult was once a child who first shyly kissed, then suddenly embraced the criminal justice system, often becoming entangled for life.

What if you grew up in a household where you never knew your father, and your mother was unable to care for you—perhaps due to an addiction—or worse, abused you physically or emotionally? Or allowed her boyfriend to do so? Or, what if you grew up in a neighborhood where the people kindest to you were gang leaders who did horrible things to others, and you were never exposed to other ways of being in the world? Who would you become? Could you even dream of a different life?

Or, what if you grew up in a world where you did not live in a home, but in a car, or were shuffled from homeless shelter to homeless shelter, school to school, shuttling between relatives? Could you focus on school, even with the best of intentions?

What if your entire society was in crisis? What if your entire childhood—all eighteen years of it—was spent in a refugee camp? Or in a country at war? What if your parents were murdered in front of you, and you were compelled to become a part of someone's army or be killed yourself? It is unfair. It is all unfair. The way that life's blessings are distributed is arbitrary and unfair. What child deserves the harshest of upbringings, and why are we surprised when that child grows up to be hard, troubled, and dangerous?

There are so many injustices in the world. I only start with those done to children because they are innately vulnerable in society. I am overwhelmed by all that should be done but have come to believe that if we each do what we can, that is better than no one doing anything.

There are meaningful ways we can contribute to the fight for social justice. We can volunteer our time to teach a child. Ironically, children are incredibly resilient. It has been shown time and time again that a single loving adult can inspire a child to dream of a different future and aspire to move beyond his or her life's circumstances. The most important element of realizing one's potential is believing that one has potential.

We can also be politically engaged. We can elect leaders who share our concern for building a society that helps those most in need. I would consider it a grave failure to have raised children who could not be bothered to vote. Every vote counts. Every election counts.

Voting is our most sacred duty as citizens and the most important way we can join with others to effect societal change. We can use the political process to provide opportunities for people who have done nothing more wrong than grow up in the wrong zip code, or city, or country. There are many examples of policies that have had a lasting generational effect: the G.I. Bill, Medicare, Medicaid, Social Security. We can and must elect leaders whose values align with our own and who are thoughtful and committed to building a more just society. I believe this is the only way to birth the policy changes that are needed.

Lastly, we can see our talent, training, and treasure as the natural outcome of investments that society has made in us and hold ourselves accountable for sharing our gifts to help others. We have a responsibility to the world we inhabit. Much has been invested in you. How will you repay it? How will you invest in others? As you have heard me say before, much is expected of those to whom much has been given.

You will always be busy. You will never feel you have time to volunteer or money to share. Your life will always feel too full to fit service into it. But the truth of the matter is, we spend our time on the things that are important to us.

If you care about people who are struggling, you will make time to show up for them in whatever way fits into your life at any given moment. My hope is that you are conscious that your privilege comes with a responsibility to help make this world work better for more people.

Doing what one can to make a difference in the lives of others is a good goal. In the end, I believe it is how we will all be judged. Did we help others? Were we kind to others? Did we try our best? It is fine and good to be successful or rack up a bunch of accomplishments, but in the end, I think what will matter most is whether we did enough to help those who needed it.

ON MEN

Women spend more time thinking about what men think than men spend actually thinking.

—Anonymous

Here's all you have to know about men and women: women are crazy, men are stupid. And the main reason women are crazy is that men are stupid.

—George Carlin

Real men don't love the most beautiful girl in the world, they love the girl who can make their world the most beautiful.

—Unknown

I am no authority on men. I know much more about women. But here is what I believe to be true.

Men are simple creatures. I don't mean that in a pejorative way, and I even admire this about them in a way. They tend to move through the world with great confidence, particularly white men, and don't even know they are doing so. Their privilege and power are invisible to them. They don't seem to worry quite as much as we do about everything. They go and do and take and don't think much of it.

Men are beautiful. Physically, of course, but also there is something wondrous about the ability of someone big and strong and powerful to be gentle. I love watching men gently play with children or carefully hold a baby. I especially enjoy watching fathers with their little girls. I love thinking about all the things raising a little girl can teach men about the women in their lives, things they perhaps never fully understood before having a daughter.

The ambition and energy of men as a force in society and human history is breathtaking. The worlds they have built, conquered, and destroyed, and the constant striving for something, bigger, better, or more seems somehow essentially male. We see it in sports too, in the desire to push to the outer limits of what is possible athletically. I'm not saying women don't have this drive. We do, for sure. But I'm admitting that when this drive is super-strong in a woman, it somehow feels like a male characteristic we happen to possess.

Men love women. If only women understood this better. They *love* us. As we are, for the most part. They are attracted to all the ways that we are different from them, as we are to them. And as much as we don't need them to do much more than be clean, they really don't require all of the things we do to make ourselves "beautiful"—perfume, makeup, shoes, clothes, nails, hair. We spend a lot of time seeking to make ourselves better somehow, changing all of the little things we perceive to be flaws, then are truly surprised at how little they notice or care.

It's not their fault. They are simple creatures. They see us physically first and foremost and tend to like what they see—with or without all the enhancements. It's a good thing.

Men are sexual creatures. Women are too, but in my view, men seem to be much more so. They cannot help but view the women they meet through a physical prism first. It doesn't mean they don't also see or care about many other wonderful aspects of women—our minds, our humor, our ideas, our concerns about the world. It just means that a woman's sexuality is always lurking somewhere in the back of their minds, and in the case of young men (i.e., college men), the front of their minds. That's okay, but it's good to be aware that for many (most?) young men, sex is the end game.

For women, sex is, at least tangentially, often linked to romance and courtship. Lurking in the background of our minds is always the pleasant possibility of a romantic, satisfying, possibly permanent, relationship. Neither description is universal, but I have found that often they are often, at least partially, true.

No matter how liberated a woman thinks she is, for many, it's just hard for us to allow someone to get that close to us, that intimate, and feel like there is no deeper connection or purpose (unless we are drunk, or otherwise impaired, but that is another chapter).

Men don't understand women. We frustrate them because we are complicated. We are indirect. We are fickle. We are particular. We have expectations for them, but we don't tell them what they are. We hope they will guess what we want, what we need from them physically, emotionally, sexually, intellectually. But men are simple creatures. It generally works best if we just tell them.

We have certain dynamics with men. We treat them like women, but they are not women. For example, sometimes when we have a problem we just want to talk out. But the man we are talking to will immediately move to help us solve it. But we don't need them to solve it. We will solve it. We just want someone to talk to about it, to explore it from all angles. To analyze the problem. We will solve it in our own good time. Which is, of course, what the women in our lives understand. But men are not women.

Another dynamic is asking for help, which women have no problem with. It does not reflect poorly on us to ask for help. Competency is really important to men, and somehow asking for help can make a man feel incompetent. It's an affront to their sense of masculinity to feel "helpless." How ridiculous. Everyone needs help, right? These are just a couple of universal dynamics that seem to repeat themselves again and again between the genders. Don't be surprised when you see it.

Men crave our approval. They want to know that we are attracted to them, that they are desirable (okay, we want this too). They want to know that we think they are capable (even if we are just as capable). They want to know we appreciate them taking care of us (even if we can take care of ourselves). Most of all, they just want to be loved (don't we all?). If we can consistently give the men in our lives these things (and sex), they will be happy. Like I said, men are simple creatures.

ON SEX

*Women need a reason to have sex. Men just
need a place.*

—Billy Crystal

One of the greatest revelations of entering adulthood is discovering our own sexuality. You've seen a lot of movies and read a lot of books about it, and popular culture is saturated with sex. It's everywhere! And it always seems like the most amazing thing ever. People fall in and out of bed all the time on TV, like its nothing. They are always having a ball.

But in real life, sex isn't "nothing." It really isn't. It's intensely personal. It's one of the most intimate things you will ever do with another human being. Good sex requires trust and communication and is enhanced by love. Good sex is selfless. Its hallmark is the sense of discovery and the excitement of taking a journey to a special place with a person you care about and experiencing that place together. It's like scuba diving: holding hands in the ocean and seeing amazing things and pointing them out to one another. It's full of passion, smiles, sighs (or screams), and sometimes chuckles. It ends with a drowsy cuddle and maybe some sleep—and the promise of future journeys to this wonderful new world you are discovering together. Sex is intertwined with and a reflection of the deepening underlying relationship. It is the culmination of the desire to get closer to someone whom you really like. It is a beautiful way to know them better and differently.

Bad sex is something else entirely—and there is plenty of it to go around. The hallmarks of bad sex are the lack of commitment the partners have to one another and a lack of communication. It may seem like it will be a good experience in the beginning. There is mutual physical attraction, so it should all work, right? But the problem is that the lack of any other rationale for having this intimate experience with someone you don't know (and may actually dislike if you took the time to know them) makes it a hollow transaction.

The assumption that it may just be a one-time thing colors the entire interaction. Each person is focused on their own wants and desires and only peripherally concerned about their partner (whom they may never see again). No one cares much about the other person's experience. It is rushed and hurried, and there is not much there at the end of it. Everyone is heading for the exits, slightly embarrassed, uninterested in having a real conversation, ready to be "away." Not very fulfilling, not very satisfying. Often a bit depressing, leaving all parties feeling worth a little bit less in the aftermath.

Regardless of how or why you end up in bed with someone, you must, must, *must* protect yourself, even as you enjoy yourself. Be on birth control. I don't think I have to tell you that this is not the time in your life to have a baby. You are presently at your most fertile (as is your partner). It will happen to you if you are not on birth control. Don't let anyone tell you different. A condom is not enough. The rhythm method is not enough. Nothing is enough to give you the certainty you need except for a real birth control method, like the pill.

While condoms are not a legitimate method of birth control, they are a highly effective way to protect you from contracting sexually transmitted diseases (STDs). Most young men these days expect to wear a condom. It should not be a big deal. HPV is rampant right now in America. It causes genital warts, and some strains cause cancer. You can get it from oral, vaginal, or anal sex. But not if you use a condom. Here is some information on HPV: https://www.cdc.gov/hpv/parents/whatishpv.html

Other diseases are common in Europe and other parts of the world. No need to have a deep conversation about it with your partner or hear his reasons why it is unnecessary, just insist. A "no condom, no sex" policy is super-smart; do *not* let someone talk you out of this, no matter how much you like them. Have condoms on hand to make it easy. You don't want to be sleeping with anyone who can't get on board with this anyway (they should be worried about contracting something from you as well).

One more thing about sex. You are in control. You are in the driver's seat. Your partner will almost always be the aggressor and you the decider of what you want to do. You must be willing to exert your will. If you are uncomfortable or want to stop or slow down, *you must say, "stop," or, "slow down," or, "no."* Your first time may be slightly uncomfortable, so take your time.

The guy you are with will be oblivious unless he explicitly hears you say "no." *Even a great guy* may miss cues that are any less subtle. He will be caught up in the experience, assuming you are enjoying it every bit as much as he is. Sex is one of the most important things you need to be honest about and communicate about clearly. To avoid being hurt. To avoid being used. To avoid being misunderstood. Don't be afraid to exert your will.

Learn to use your voice to express your preferences. What you like and don't like. Don't be embarrassed, just be clear. You will probably have a few (several?) different partners in life. They may be fairly experienced lovers or just starting out. In both cases, they won't know your body.

You may not know your body. Learn about it. You should orgasm when you have sex. If you do not, your partner just hasn't learned how to help a woman orgasm yet. Teach him. Read up on it if you can't figure it out.

Men are easy. Anything you do will be appreciated. They are just so happy to be there! They are very direct and very comfortable expressing their wants and needs; you need to do the same.

Sex is for pleasure. The hidden capacity of our bodies to yield pleasure is a powerful discovery.

Enjoy!

Safely.

ON MONEY

Not everything that can be counted, counts, and not everything that counts can be counted.

—Albert Einstein

I'm not going to lie. It's nice to have enough money to have and do the things you want to do in life. But it's not everything. I am grateful that I have lived both ways: with enough and without. I understand that not having enough—from the time I left home, in college, after graduating, living in New York, and my first few years in

Minneapolis—shaped the decisions I made to create a life in which I would have enough.

I often wonder what my ambition would have been if I had never worked while I was in Hawaii or if I had never struggled financially in my early 20s. I remember being strapped for cash and thinking, *Oh, no. This is not how I want to live. I want to go and see and do whatever I want, whenever I want. I don't want to pinch pennies my whole life and deprive myself of the things that bring me pleasure.*

But as I became more financially secure, I began to understand that money was necessary, but not sufficient. In my early twenties, I worked very hard, as hard as it took to be outstanding, to distinguish myself in business school and at General Mills, and my career flourished. But at a certain point, while I had friends and family and even a boyfriend or two along the way, I began to become fearful that I would end up alone in life. Comfortable financially, but alone. And I began to make more of an effort to try to meet that special person I could share my life and build a family with.

I am grateful that I figured this out. There are many women whom I have met over the years who are my age and very successful in their careers, but either intentionally or unintentionally have found themselves alone. Without a partner or kids to enjoy the fruits of their labor. It is certainly not the end of the world, and on good days has its advantages, for sure, but it gets less interesting, I think, as you age, and as you begin to understand all of the experiences you won't have. Being alone in your sixties, seventies, and eighties is not on your mind in your twenties and thirties, but life becomes very different based on the choices you make. Just look at the joyful life Grandma and Grandpa lead flitting around the world for birthday parties, recitals, performances, graduations—whatever is going on within the wonderful, growing family they have created.

Money should be the outcome of doing something you are passionate about, not the goal itself. The best choices you will make for your professional life are those that allow you to do work that you actually enjoy. Work during which time stands still, where you find yourself looking up and realizing that somehow four hours have gone by. You were so engrossed in what you were doing that you didn't notice; you were in the so-called "flow." You should be motivated, proud, and excited by your work. It should be work you might even consider doing for free. If you can get into that space, the money will come, and your day-to-day work life will be fulfilling.

The other important thing to know about money is that it's not how much you make that counts, it's how much you spend. Our financial planner once told your father and me that he has many clients making millions of dollars who live hand-to-mouth. They struggle financially because they are unable to budget. They spend money as fast as they make it on non-appreciating material assets (cars, fancy jewelry, clothes, etc.), and they don't save anything. They think the money will never run out. Or maybe they just don't think about it much at all.

One thing your father has really done an amazing job of, is making sure that we are always saving. Get into the habit of putting a third of your paycheck into a savings account each pay period to keep building your nest egg. If you can't do a third, do a quarter. If you can't do a quarter, do 10 percent. You should never do less than 10 percent. Avoid eating into your nest egg at all costs. Grow it!

If you work for a company with a 401K plan, you *always* want to max this amazing asset out. We can't believe the idiots that don't use this simple vehicle for saving that so many companies provide. You set aside a certain percentage of each paycheck to be direct-deposited into your 401K when you start with a company, and from that point on, year in and year out, as you are promoted and your income grows, that percentage gets automatically taken out of your paycheck and put into this account on a pre-tax basis. You never miss it, but it is quietly accumulating over the years, securing your future. Depending on the company, sometimes some of what you save is actually *matched* by your employer based on company performance. I am not making this up. Free money. It may not feel like much at first, but over time it is a simple, painless way to accumulate significant wealth. But you will also want to save some amount of your paycheck *on top* of a 401K.

Investing is particularly potent if you start early because money, even applying a very modest interest rate, compounds so powerfully over time. My advice is to invest the bulk of your money in the stock of companies whose products or services you know and love and avoid making a lot of portfolio changes (and incurring a lot of fees). Avoid chasing the "hot tip" or the exciting new start-up your friend told you about and stick with industry leading medium and large cap companies that have been successful over time, in industries that are going to be with us for the foreseeable future. Remember, by the time you hear about the "hot tip", it is very likely lukewarm at best.

I'm not suggesting that you should not have any exposure to growth in your portfolio, only that it should be balanced with a mix of lower risk investments. Professional assistance is a great idea if you lack either time or interest in building your own investment expertise. It is less important that you invest a lot of money, than that you keep adding to the pool of money you are investing. Lastly, I would recommend that you build a diversified portfolio that spans several industries and never let anyone persuade you to gamble your entire nest egg on "a sure bet". These never seem to turn out as planned. Slow and steady wins the race because time is on your side.

I would also encourage you to give away some of your money. We give away 10 percent of our income each year. We give to charities doing work in the community that we believe in, mostly around education. You will have your own favorites that align with your passions. Don't worry if the amount is small, it will grow over time.

Always keep a budget, so you know how much you have coming in after tax, how much you need to spend to survive (rent, utilities, car payment, food), how much you want to spend to "play" (movies, restaurants, clothes, hair, nails, etc.), how much you want to save, and how much you want to give away. If you have self-discipline, keep a written-down budget, save money, and don't buy things you can't afford, you will be very successful at accumulating wealth—no matter what your salary is. Effective money management is an essential life skill that will pay dividends (literally) throughout your life.

I didn't start getting my hair and nails done until after I had you guys. I did it myself because I couldn't afford to do otherwise. Having the discipline to live within your means, or better yet, *under* your means, will ensure you always have enough to be comfortable in life. Restaurants are expensive. Starbucks is expensive. Be smart with your money, and you will have enough to live the way you want one day. Spend it unwisely, and you will never feel like you have enough. And you will be right. If you place no limits on what you will spend, by definition, you will never have enough, no matter how much money you make.

A word about credit cards. They are dangerous. You are most vulnerable in the ten years right out of college. You will have a lot of new expenses, and it's tempting to put them on a credit card and carry a balance. But the interest rates credit cards charge consumers to "float" their debt are some of the highest out there. It's absolutely stupid to pay these exorbitant rates—and things can get out of control very quickly.

By the way, there is no point in saving if you are paying interest to a credit card company because the interest rate differential (between what you are being charged for your credit card debt versus what you could make with savings or investment) is so unfavorable. It would be like running backward (not even in place). First, pay down your credit card debt, then save.

Many young people get into serious trouble with credit cards and ruin their credit (the financial rating that enables you to make large purchases like a car or apartment or washing machine). What they don't know is that once you ruin your credit, it becomes very challenging to make large purchases. Do not do this.

Debt is a challenge in general when you are young. I had significant undergraduate and graduate student loans when I was in my 20s and 30s. I always paid my debt, but it certainly wasn't easy and I leaned heavily on credit cards. I never got in arrears and did not trash my credit, but I will never forget my mortification at explaining $10,000 worth of credit card debt I would be bringing into our marriage after your father proposed to me. Don't make this mistake. Buy what you can afford, and pay the balance at the end of each month. Basic personal financial management is an essential life skill.

Your father and I often reflect that we are lucky that we know what is really important in life: the people we get to share it with—our family and our friends. It is finding time to help others. It's taking time to go for a walk together with the dog. It's sitting in front of a fire at the lake. It's laying blankets down on the deck of our cabin and looking up at the stars on a pitch-black night. It's sharing a simple meal together and catching up on the events of the day. It's participating as a productive member of society. Most of all, it's nurturing the next generation—you and your sister, and whatever other young people we can impact positively along the way.

We also know that if for some reason the resources we have accumulated went away, we could downscale our lives and live very modestly without complaint. We understand that, as Grandpa Jones always says, "All honest work, done well, is honorable." We are not too precious to do what we need to do to support ourselves and our family. If I needed to work at a McDonald's, I would, and it would be just fine. I'd be a passionate, committed worker with a great attitude, and I would be grateful for that job if it was the only one I could get. Work is a blessing. Being able to support oneself is a blessing.

The most important thing to remember about money is that while it is an important enabler in life, it is only one of many things that will allow you to live the life you dream of, and it is not the most important one by a longshot.

ON FORGIVENESS

Consider the rights of others before your own feelings, and the feelings of others before your own rights.

—Coach John Wooden

One of the greatest character traits you can cultivate is the ability to forgive others. When people hurt us, our natural instinct is to lash out and hurt them back. This is normal, but not very productive or helpful. Whether a loved one says something that hurts your feelings, a colleague undermines you at work or a stranger cuts you off in traffic, it is very hard to just let it go. And yet, there is generally very little to be gained through retaliation and often quite a bit to lose. For so many situations, the right response it to simply shake it off and move on.

When it's a loved one who has wounded you, you can try being honest and simply let them know how much they hurt you. Escalating the situation by attacking them tends to make things worse. By the way, sometimes loved ones say hurtful things that are important for us to hear. For a challenging colleague, their behavior is simply an indication of who they are and that they cannot be trusted, good knowledge for you to tuck away for the future. When it's a stranger, you might consider thinking about whatever is going on in their life that may be producing the intensity of their wrath. It often seems such individuals live their lives with rage simmering just below the surface, ready to bubble over at the slightest provocation. Their ire is likely less about other people's driving skills and more about whatever is happening in their lives.

The ability to forgive is a sign of great maturity. It means you are able to put your needs and sense of grievance aside. It means your life is sufficiently abundant that you can be emotionally generous with others. Emotional generosity means understanding that many petty things are simply not worth fighting over. You can actively choose not to engage in silly conflict. You can choose, instead, to bring a positive spirit to challenging interactions.

Forgiveness is inextricably bound up in conflict resolution. Conflict is an essential part of the human experience: two children in a sandbox, two men fighting over the same woman, two countries fighting over the same useless strip of land. It's all the same thing at its core. Conflict cannot be avoided, so it is wise to get good at conflict resolution. I would argue that this simple skill can be one of the most useful you will ever acquire.

It helps that many, though not all, conflicts are actually misunderstandings. And many, though not all, conflicts can be resolved by listening to one another and applying a little bit of empathy, understanding, creativity, and forgiveness.

Resolving conflict well requires being sufficiently creative to imagine new possible outcomes. Central to most conflicts is the belief that there can only be one outcome; either the outcome party A wants or the one that party B wants. Great conflict resolution comes from seeing that there are actually eight additional outcomes that parties A and B could both live with, none of them ideal, but all of them acceptable. And so, the process of conflict resolution is one of exploration and discovery: How do we find those additional outcomes that could work, albeit imperfectly? Sounds basic, but we generally lose all sense of creativity when we are angry. We screw down more tightly on our position and become unwilling to entertain the concerns of the opposing side. Many people cannot move away from their anger or their righteous sense of injury. This fundamental inability can permeate people's lives and make them resentful and unpleasant to be around. It's a bit of an indulgence, really, and laziness in thinking. Pity-party thinking.

The skill of being able to step back, cool off, think clearly, and then begin to brainstorm how to tease out a new solution is extremely useful. The willingness to ignore hurtful words expressed in anger, to understand that they were not really meant and to forgive the fact that they were spoken, will stand you in good stead in this world.

ON RACE

No one can make you feel inferior without your consent.

—Eleanor Roosevelt

No one is born hating another person because of the color of his skin, or his background, or his religion. People must learn to hate, and if they can learn to hate, they can be taught to love, for love comes more naturally to the human heart than its opposite.

—Nelson Mandela

If you grow up black in America, at some point in your life you will have to make your peace with the skin you are in. It helps if the external world perceives you to be both smart and beautiful (as it will perceive you). But even then, it can be a slow and painful journey to self-acceptance.

We have spoken of race many times over the years, but I know better than most that it's different to talk about a thing like this than to go out into the world and experience it. My guess is that you will be mercifully oblivious to many slights, as I was. You will subconsciously make excuses for things that others who are more schooled in the nuances of these things would understand right away. Sometimes ignorance is bliss, and I sort of hope you won't notice racism when it comes calling for you, and when you do, you won't care.

I am reminded of a story your father tells of how Grandma Valerie was once "blacklisted" when she moved into a new neighborhood in Minnetonka because of some unintended, unknown transgression against the street's queen bee. The funny part is that she was completely unaware of it! She found out years later and just laughed and laughed at the busybodies who thought they were "excluding" her, because she never even noticed. This is a good way to be as we think about race.

Of course, sometimes it's not possible to ignore the very real consequences of being excluded because of one's race. Not being hired, promoted or developed in the same ways as one's peers is hard to ignore and even harder to pin on racism with certainty. But we don't get to control these things. What we can control is our own effort, the positive energy and engagement we bring to our endeavors and our commitment to doing our best ever day. Strong performance tends to trump all else because, as my friend Westina Matthews always says, "The color is green, the color is green, the color is green." Organizations value employees that contribute to the bottom line. Try to focus all of your energy there and let the rest sort itself out.

There are, of course, positives and negatives in the way that race may play out for you on campus. I understand that I am just going by my own experience and it may be different for you. You will have to discover your own truth, but here are some possibilities for you to think about.

The good news is you will always have access to the African American community. This community will always claim you. The bad news is that sometimes you will feel not fully a part of it. Your African American peers will hail from every point on the socio-economic spectrum and from high schools of varying degrees of diversity. These differences will shape how you and your peers perceive the college environment. Mainstream colleges will feel comfortable and normal to those who have come from predominantly white high schools and quite challenging to those who haven't.

One of the unintended consequences of growing up in Minnesota is that you have lived in a white world your whole life. As much as we have tried to elevate and celebrate black culture, expose you to black people (i.e. through friends, my family and church) and ensure you are proud of that part of yourself, the fact is, you have not gone to a predominantly black school or lived in a predominantly black community. This is part of why you may experience the sensation of being both "a part of" and "not a part of" the black community.

We chose the high school you attended because it offered the very best education we could afford. We also liked the way it values and celebrates diversity and multiculturalism. We thought this support would be important, raising biracial kids in the middle of a very white state. Your school was not perfect and did not get race right in many ways, but it aspired to, and you will understand how special your experience was as you get some distance from it.

Some of your African American peers will be grappling with being a minority on a predominantly white campus. My guess is that you won't feel that particular anxiety in the same way. You are more likely to feel that you can go, do, and be yourself wherever and however you want—as you always have. You may be a bit taken aback the first time you sense that not everyone sees you as you see yourself.

You won't feel many constraints associated with race, and it may surprise you to find that some of your African American peers do. Some may have an "us versus them" mindset. It is only what they have grown up with and experienced in life. It may surprise you that they will sometimes assign motives or make assumptions or interpret things that happen in a racialized way that would never have occurred to you. Sometimes they will be right, and sometimes they will be wrong, but the point is you might never have even gone there. You will listen to them quietly, but inside you might be thinking, *Wow, I really don't think it was that deep.* Occasionally you may speak up to provide a possible different interpretation, but you may feel obliged to do so less and less over time as you realize it's just a difference in worldview, or as you begin to realize how many times they are right.

For some of your black peers, other African Americans at school will feel like a lifeline where they can finally let down their guard and relax. In some ways, being in a predominantly white (or at least non-black) school will be like living in a different country for them, with a different language, cultural norms, foods, customs, beliefs about the world, etc. Their college years will be invaluable to them for this alone. They will need to learn how to make their way in this environment, which mimics all of the major structures of power in the society they will confront when they graduate—business, government, non-profit, etc.—all largely dominated by white people. You will have your fair share of social challenges, for sure, but not being comfortable with white kids is not likely to be one of them.

Your challenge may be understanding where you fit in within the black community. Ironically, being biracial and having grown up with a mix of kids grants you access to both black and white communities but doesn't guarantee you will fully fit into either. You may feel neither fish nor fowl, not black enough nor white enough. At first, anyway. Give it time.

You will make friends of all genders and ethnicities, and as they get to know your brilliant, wonderful self, all the noise of race will fall away. Everyone brings their life experiences to the table. Yours are no better or worse than anyone else's. Everyone is trying to make friends and fit into a new social order. Be patient. Let people get to know you. All will be well.

It will be a good thing for all of you—with your diverse experiences—to connect and get to know one another. My guess is that you will form strong friendships with black students in college and I hope you seek out the campus Black Student Union to begin that journey of figuring out the role race will play in your life.

This is how it was for me when I went from Hawaii to Georgetown. I had no problem with the majority of the white community. The challenge was figuring out how to be a part of, but not exclusively defined by, the black community. I wanted to be myself and make friends with whomever I wanted and go to whatever parties or events I wanted—and that is what I did. I found my way, as you will find yours, and just made friends in all places. I did some things with the black community but didn't let it constrain me as I observed it did some of my black peers.

However you experience race at college, your understanding of what it means for you and the world you are a part of will deepen over the next four years. It may cause you occasional heartache (or headache), as you may find yourself defined by and judged for your race by both the black and white community, but ultimately, it won't be a big deal.

This may all be different for you, but no one ever told me what to expect, and I experienced quite a bit of culture shock navigating race in college. So, I just thought I would share my thoughts and experiences, and you can take the best and leave the rest. I am not sure how much of a difference it would have made if someone had told me what to expect. Perhaps these are things that we each must grapple with in our own way.

ON GRATITUDE

Be thankful for what you have; you'll end up having more. If you concentrate on what you don't have, you will never, ever have enough.

—Oprah Winfrey

Let gratitude be the starting point of each day. Let gratitude wash over you as you close your eyes each night. And when you find yourself with a moment of quiet in the midst of a busy day, let gratitude be your resting point. For you have much to be grateful for, and gratitude breeds both humility and a striving to earn all that has been given to you.

"The word gratitude is derived from the Latin word gratia, which means grace, graciousness, or gratefulness (depending on the context). In some ways gratitude encompasses all of these meanings. Gratitude is a thankful appreciation for what an individual receives, whether tangible or intangible. With gratitude, people acknowledge the goodness in their lives. In the process, people usually recognize that the source of that goodness lies at least partially outside themselves. As a result, gratitude also helps people connect to something larger than themselves as individuals—whether to other people, nature, or a higher power."[1] This is from Harvard Medical School and is therefore a perspective grounded in science, not religion. You would do well to take note.

There has actually been quite a bit of research done on the link between gratitude and happiness. Lest you think I am making this up, below is more from Harvard Medical School:

"Two psychologists, Dr. Robert A. Emmons of the University of California, Davis, and Dr. Michael E. McCullough of the University of Miami, have done much of the research on gratitude. In one study, they asked all participants to write a few sentences each week, focusing on particular topics.

One group wrote about things they were grateful for that had occurred during the week. A second group wrote about daily irritations or things that had displeased them, and the third wrote about events that had affected them (with no emphasis on them being positive or negative). After 10 weeks, those who wrote about gratitude were more optimistic and felt better about their lives. Surprisingly, they also exercised more and had fewer visits to physicians than those who focused on sources of aggravation.

Another leading researcher in this field, Dr. Martin E. P. Seligman, a psychologist at the University of Pennsylvania, tested the impact of various positive psychology interventions on 411 people, each compared with a control assignment of writing about early memories. When their week's assignment was to write and personally deliver a letter of gratitude to someone who had never been properly thanked for his or her kindness, participants immediately exhibited a huge increase in happiness scores.

This impact was greater than that from any other intervention, with benefits lasting for a month.

Of course, studies such as this one cannot prove cause and effect. But most of the studies published on this topic support an association between gratitude and an individual's well-being. Other studies have looked at how gratitude can improve relationships. For example, a study of couples found that individuals who took time to express gratitude for their partner not only felt more positive toward the other person but also felt more comfortable expressing concerns about their relationship.

Managers who remember to say "thank you" to people who work for them may find that those employees feel motivated to work harder. Researchers at the Wharton School at the University of Pennsylvania randomly divided university fundraisers into two groups. One group made phone calls to solicit alumni donations in the same way they always had. The second group—assigned to work on a different day—received a pep talk from the director of annual giving, who told the fundraisers she was grateful for their efforts. During the following week, the university employees who heard her message of gratitude made 50% more fundraising calls than those who did not."[1]

I found this research interesting because it confirms what I have observed in my life watching people like my own father move through the world with a profound sense of optimism and gratitude. I aspire to do the same each day and hope you will too.

---

[1] In Praise of Gratitude. (June 5, 2019). Harvard Mental Health Newsletter, Harvard Health Publishing, Harvard Medical School, June 5, 2019.
https://www.health.harvard.edu/mind-and-mood/in-praise-of-gratitude

ON EDUCATION

Education is the most powerful weapon which you can use to change the world.

—Nelson Mandela

E ducation is the great liberator. It frees us from the shackles of our own limited imaginations. It shatters beliefs previously held sacrosanct. It causes our mental landscape to constantly shift and reconfigure to accommodate inconvenient new truths and to adapt to realities inconsistent with our own experience. Healthy people are lifelong learners who are unafraid to learn they were wrong and who seek out the seductive siren of truth, wherever it may lead them. They are not satisfied to "know." They want to know *more*, know *better*, know *differently*.

I know you understand the value of education. You have been living it your whole life. But I also hope you understand the joy of learning. Learning, not to get a grade or to complete an assignment, but to follow your own intellectual curiosity.

The next four years will mark a transition in your educational experience. Up until now you went to school because, well, that's what you had always done. It's the law. It was also our pleasure and desire, as your parents, that you do so. In high school, maybe you felt that studying hard was about nothing more than getting into college. But now you are nineteen, and you get to decide where learning fits into the rest of your life. You have this amazing opportunity to explore your interests for four whole years. To discover what excites you, to expose yourself to new areas of inquiry, to stay up late arguing with your peers, and to engage your professors in debate. You will grow so much, intellectually and emotionally, over this time.

It is my hope that along the way, the fire is lit, and you carry the torch for learning forward into the rest of your life. Wherever you go, whatever you do, there is more to learn. Let it be a passion and a joy!

The acquisition of knowledge isn't just about knowing things. It's about applying your knowledge to solve challenges or create new opportunities, which is how you contribute to the world. Whether your passion is art or theater or mathematics or genetics or sociology, inquiry into an area of interest is where the sparks fly. Meeting people who are interested in the same areas of inquiry is one of life's great joys. Do not miss this!

ON LONELINESS

Embracing human frailty, fallibility, and heartbreaking aloneness is crucial for any person seeking to attain self-actualization and self-realization.

—Kilroy J. Oldster

Some journeys in life can only be traveled alone.

—Ken Poirot

There is a difference between being alone and being lonely. Being alone, for many of us, is a refreshing tonic—a kind of peace and solace within the hysteria of our world. A chance to close into the comfort of oneself, to explore quietly at our own pace whatever is before us, wrapped in the warm and cozy blanket of solitude. This is the way of introverts—I know this from experience.

But this indulgence, left unchecked, can morph into loneliness, for we are communal creatures not meant to be too much alone. Loneliness is a sort of self-enforced aloneness. There is no reason to be lonely. It takes very little effort to join with others. It is a choice. It may dawn on us, in those times of loneliness, that we might actually appreciate the company of another—to go see a movie or grab a bite to eat—but there is not a viable option in sight. Sometimes it is because, as introverts, we have simply failed in the basic task of friendship cultivation. We've said "no" too many times when invited to participate in this or that event. Sometimes it's because we may have an innate aloofness, or a social impatience, or a sense of always being awkward or apart or different. Sometimes it's an intolerance for the niceties of small talk. Sometimes it is painful shyness.

No matter. The point is that we are all lonely lots of times in our lives. Part of growing up is learning to move through loneliness and rediscover our choice in the matter. As in most things, we are the masters of our destiny here and can always make the choice to reach out to others. We can rekindle old friendships, nurture new acquaintances, take that first step to ask someone to do something with us, or insert ourselves into settings where we can reach out and make new friends. College is the ideal setting for making new friends, and many of them will become lifelong. That doesn't mean that you won't sometimes want to be alone.

The other thing to pay attention to is becoming homesick. If you feel sad and adrift, like no one knows you enough to care deeply about you, it is only because you are away from the people who love you most and the familiarity of all you have known. It is perfectly normal and to be expected. It would be strange if you never did miss home. These sad feelings will pass. You are creating a new home for yourself as part of the campus community, and it will be wonderful!

ON TECHNOLOGY

It has become appallingly obvious that our technology has exceeded our humanity.

— Albert Einstein

I am conscious of the irony of my opining on technology. I could possibly be the least qualified person to offer any insights or relevant thoughts on this topic. And yet, I find I do have thoughts to share (surprise!).

Technology is the great transformer that has propelled humankind forward from the start. From figuring out how to create fire on demand, to inventing and utilizing the wheel for transportation, to manufacturing tools, to building machines to make our lives easier, it is our nature as human beings to seek a better way.

The natural consequence of this innate drive to improve our natural environment has culminated in the hyper-automated, hyper-connected, hyper-digital world that you have grown up in. Unlike previous generations, you know nothing of a past where there was no alternative to the messy, often embarrassing, sometimes humiliating ubiquity of face-to-face, one-on-one interaction.

It is a weakness, I believe, to misunderstand the importance and centrality of direct human interaction to our quality of life. We need to be connected to one another both physically and emotionally *directly*. We need to live the vulnerability of sharing what we really believe in our souls—verbally, in person. And if we have something negative or hard to say to someone, we need to learn how to say it—to their face.

The protective shield of anonymity that shrouds the internet is beguiling but can be dangerous to us as individuals and to our society. There are consequences to what we say, but we are not always held accountable for our digital commentary. The internet allows people to say and do things they would not publicly. Everything you say or do on the internet you should be comfortable having people you love and respect read. As in real life, respect and courtesy go a long way.

The other caution about technology is the insidious way it leads us to passive, inward-facing interactions with screens (phones, computers, video games, televisions)—for *hours*. When we are interacting with technology, we are not enjoying the company of others, the beauty of nature, live entertainment, or the wonder of love. We are not creating something new, unique, and special in the real world. We are just staring at a machine, really. A lot of time can pass that is ultimately spent sitting still, staring at a bunch of pixels. Years, in fact. We only have so many of those, by the way. Time is the currency of our lives, and we should be judicious about how we spend it.

Technology is increasingly taking a toll on relationships. Being engaged with a screen versus the person sitting right next to you is the ultimate rejection. It says, "What I am doing on my screen right now is infinitely more interesting and important than interacting directly with you. The people I am texting, the show I am watching, the information I am looking up, are very, very important—and you are less so."

The other concern about technology is the way it eats our brains. Passively taking in information on a screen is vastly different than, say, reading a book. There is no imagination to apply, nothing to create—it's all there for you already. You have only to look to digest what someone has already baked. Some amount of digital consumption is just fine, but too much is debilitating.

There is an addictive quality to technology that is particularly concerning. There are many studies showing the harmful effects of technology on children. Part of it is the actual consumption of technology (e.g., time spent, content consumed), but part of it is the things that kids are *not* doing as a consequence of the time spent with technology (e.g., running around outside, creating make-believe games, reading, writing, playing).

One of the greatest concerns with the rise in use of technology—especially amongst young people—is the decline in reading. Reading a book requires us to translate words into made-up mental images that we can literally "see" in our mind's eye. These images are not static; they contain three-dimensional beings that interact in the world they inhabit, complete with emotions and experiences. All of this is from looking at some black markings on a white page. The feat of reading is marvelous and wonderful. The act of reading is mind-opening—we can go anywhere in this world or any world, sitting still with a book in our hands. You have always loved to read for pleasure. Do not lose this affection. Books have always been one of the most satisfying diversions in my life. I hope it is the same for you.

The last thing I will say about technology is how it pertains to work. Technology has, of course, transformed the workplace, ushering in the previously unknown freedom of working when and where we want. The dark side of this freedom is that it is terribly easy to be working, literally, all of the time, because our work tools are always with us. Learning how to shut off work so that we can enjoy downtime away from it will be one of your greatest professional challenges.

Another thing to watch out for in this digital era relates to employment. Your digital footprint is easily accessible and diligently investigated by potential employers as a matter of routine. You really must assume that nothing you say in social media is private, and that if it is discoverable, it will be discovered. Even seemingly mild or innocuous conversations online may be seen as inappropriate in the eyes of a future employer. It is a brave new world when it comes to hiring, and as digital natives it's important to understand this.

All of this is not to say that technology is bad. It is actually quite wonderful! We need technology, and it is life-enhancing for sure—for entertainment, for tracking down the information we need, for socializing with friends, and for keeping up with what is happening around the world. Technology is indispensable and enabling, but we should take care and make sure we are using it in moderation and not to the exclusion of the other wonderful things the world has on offer for us to experience.

ON MARRIAGE

A great marriage is not when the "perfect couple" comes together. It is when an imperfect couple learns to enjoy their differences.

—Dave Meurer

If I get married, I want to be very married.

—Audrey Hepburn

Marriage is on the outs these days. Monogamy is unfashionable.

Many in your generation pooh-pooh the piece of paper, are uninspired by the idea of a permanent commitment, and disdain the religious undertones of the institution. After all, institutions are, well, institutional, and therefore uninteresting by definition.

As you head off to college, it will no doubt feel like that educational choice is the most significant decision you will make in your life, but you would be wrong. In fact, the most consequential decision you will make in your life will be your choice of a life partner.

You don't get to choose your parents or family, but your life partner is on you. This individual, if you get it right, is likely to share your life's journey longer than even your parents. They will celebrate every major event in your life, share your joys, and commiserate with you on every setback. They will be silly with you, serious with you, laugh, cry, sing, dance, love, and experience the most magnificent moments of your life with you. Most importantly, you may share the most awesome and life-changing experience two people can: raising children together. Choose wisely.

Of course, the most important part of your choice is the alignment of values between you and your prospective partner. I don't believe a marriage can truly be successful if partners have different core values. You can (will and should) have different personalities, pleasures, preferences, priorities, but values are the underlying beliefs about what matters most in how we live our lives. Values embody the underlying principles that guide our behavior every day and determine how we treat those around us. If your core values are truly misaligned, it is unlikely the match will work over time.

Here are a few other things that matter:

-Feeling mutual physical attraction
-Feeling satisfied even when doing nothing together while in the same room
-Finding it easy to be together, not stressful or awkward
-Feeling you can be yourself and be loved for who you are—at your worst
-Feeling supported

The keys to a successful marriage are mutual kindness, enjoying each other's company (even when you aren't really doing anything), and communication. If you get the values right and work on these three things, you'll be fine.

I can't believe next year will mark twenty-seven years of marriage for your father and me. It went fast. We've always had fun together, and we've enjoyed planning and dreaming together. We've tried to respect one another—you've never seen us scream or swear at each other or call each other names. That sort of ugly behavior doesn't sit well with either of us (we actually don't care to behave that way toward anyone, let alone each other).

Learning how to resolve conflicts is essential in a strong marriage. Conflict is inevitable. You are two different people with different wants, needs, and desires. So how do you work through these differences to find what works best for both of you? Negotiation. Give and take. Indulgence. Kindness. Generosity. Maturity. Never go to sleep angry. Learn how to make up after a fight—usually it just takes one of you to be "big" about the situation.

As a matter of fact, learn how to fight. When emotions run high it is easy to say hurtful things you don't mean but can never take back. Learn how to avoid crossing lines that should not be crossed. Learn how to control your irritation and bring a generous spirit to your relationship. I guess it's all just practice, like most things you want to do well.

There are always forces eating away at a marriage. People can grow in different directions. Petty resentments can accumulate over the years. The "power relationship" can get out of whack, creating a situation where one partner does not feel equal to the other. In sum, lack of care and feeding. A marriage is a garden of delights that must be tended carefully to be enjoyed.

I'm so glad to have married your father. He is the most kind, generous, and wonderful man I know—but you're already aware of that! They say that girls marry their fathers—I certainly hope that is the case for you. You would be lucky to find someone with some of the wonderful qualities of your father. He has set a high bar, but I suspect that you will have great judgment as you select a mate. My guess is that you will be quite picky, but when the right person comes along, they will sweep you off your feet. You'll know they are the one.

ON MOTHERHOOD

Babies are bits of star-dust blown from the hand of God. Lucky the woman who knows the pangs of birth for she has held a star.

—Larry Barretto

Whatever else is unsure in this stinking dunghill of a world a mother's love is not.

—James Joyce

H mmm. It's probably a bit early to be writing this chapter. Never mind.

ON SELF-DISCIPLINE

I count him braver who overcomes his desires than him who conquers his enemies, for the hardest victory is victory over self.

—Aristotle

One of the greatest skills to cultivate is the ability to do what needs to be done. Sounds simple, but it's not. There are endless distractions pushing and pulling at us, demanding our attention, preventing us from doing the things we need to do. The things you might want to do could range from working out, eating right, sleeping, studying, getting homework assignments done, reading a book—whatever. The distractions could be friends, things happening on campus, inertia, gaming, TV, junk food, laziness, sleepiness, parties, friends, good weather—you name it.

Self-discipline allows you to balance enjoying delightful distractions and sticking to your plan. You are the only person in the world who can impose your will in these matters. You will need to recognize when you are getting off track and course-correct. You are the only one who can get yourself to the gym, who can avoid overindulging in the cafeteria, who can show up to class or to a study group prepared. You are in the driver's seat, and self-discipline is all about taking ahold of the wheel and driving where you want to go, not aimlessly wandering around on cruise control.

You have exercised excellent self-discipline thus far in your life, demonstrated by your successful high school career, but beware, the unstructured college environment has derailed many perfectly well-organized, dedicated high school students. Think about the strategies you can employ to stay on track. Your high school did a wonderful job leading you through the process of managing your assignments in a planner over the course of your years there. Take this habit with you into college and beyond. You have excellent study skills. You know that you have to start early with review, and you know how to create the learning aids that work best for you. But it's easy to become distracted.

If you get off track, just get back on track. The sooner you start, the sooner you can get things back under control. If you really start to fall behind, reach out and get help. There are resources in college available to assist you. A daily written schedule that incorporates work, play, and anything in between is an extremely good thing to have. College should not be all work and no play—it's important to schedule in the fun stuff, too!

Time is the currency of your life; spend it wisely.

ON INTEGRITY

Right is right, even if everyone is against it, and wrong is wrong, even if everyone is for it.

—William Penn

Be more concerned with your character than your reputation, because your character is what you really are, while your reputation is merely what others think you are.

—Coach John Wooden

Integrity is living your values even when no one is looking. When no one will ever know if you did the right thing or not. Only you. Integrity is the foundation of trust. It reflects the consistency of ethical behavior in an individual. High-integrity people are worthy of our trust. You can trust a person of high integrity to always be honest with you, to not steal or lie or cheat, to behave honorably in all settings. You would trust such a person with important job responsibilities. You would trust them with your possessions. You would trust them with your children.

There is a discipline to high-integrity individuals, a self-policing. They do what is right because it is right, not because they are afraid of getting caught doing something wrong. They are resistant to distortions of the truth, a good thing to aspire to.

Your reputation is a reflection of your integrity, the shadow it casts. In many respects, it's all you have. Once it is trashed, it can never quite be put back together the way it was. It is worth protecting.

Lastly, people of high integrity tend to attract others who are similarly concerned with what is right versus what is convenient or popular or easy. You will know these people when you meet them. They are good people to surround yourself with.

ON PERSISTENCE

First they ignore you, then they laugh at you, then they fight you, then you win.

Gandhi

So much of what makes people successful in life is their ability to persevere in the face of adversity. Persistence is at the center of skill acquisition; to get good at anything you have to stick with it long enough for the practice to pay off. A part of persistence is patience. The willingness to wait. The understanding that the best things in life often take time to create, experience, and enjoy.

Persistence is about a steady and continuous application of effort over time. It reflects an understanding of the path to mastery of virtually everything. There is an often quoted saying, "Fools rush in where angels fear to tread," which is in reference to a poem written by the English poet, Alexander Pope, in 1709 called "An Essay on Criticism." In my mind, the meaning is that inexperienced people will often be in a hurry to do, see, experience, and try. They rush to do things when wiser people take a more measured approach. They are playing the long game and willing to make the investment to win it.

A close cousin to persistence is resiliency. Resiliency is the ability to bounce back from defeat or failure. Defeat and failure are not great experiences for anyone, but for some, these twin terrors are crushing. Debilitating. Some people just can't get past a failure. They relive the experience over and over in their minds, agonizing over what they could have said or done differently. They mope and moan about things that are in the past and struggle to simply let them go.

Internalizing the negative feelings failure produces can profoundly impact your self-esteem. The opportunity is to understand that there is always a positive in failure. What is the positive? You get to learn something new and you get to try again. In most cases, failures help us to learn how do better the next time. Resilient people keep this knowledge close and grab ahold of it to pull themselves back up on their feet when something goes wrong in life. And something always goes wrong at some point in our lives.

Another trait that helps us to persist is flexibility. It is helpful to live life with a sense that there are many possibilities to every situation that will produce equally rewarding outcomes—even if they are not the outcomes we initially expected or worked for. Your father often recounts a Chinese parable he once heard called, "Good Luck, Bad Luck:"

There once was a farmer who used an old mare to till his fields.

One day, the mare ran away, disappearing into the surrounding hills. When the farmer's neighbors sympathized with the old man over his bad luck, the farmer replied, "Bad luck? Good luck? Who knows?"

A week later, the mare returned, followed by a herd of horses from the hills, including a beautiful black stallion. This time the neighbors congratulated the farmer on his good luck at having obtained such wealth. His reply was "Good luck? Bad luck? Who knows?"

The next week when the farmer's son was attempting to ride the stallion, he fell off the horse and broke his leg. The neighbors all commiserated with the farmer on this very bad luck. The farmer's reaction: "Bad luck? Good luck? Who knows?"

Some weeks later, the army arrived and conscripted every able-bodied young male in the village to fight in a war. But the farmer's son's leg was broken, and so he was not taken.

Good luck or bad luck? Who knows?

And so, the story continues. The point is, we don't know how what is happening at any given point in our lives is connected to our future. It behooves us to treat it all with an adventurous spirit and trust that it will all come out right in the end. Approaching life with a little flexibility helps us accept unexpected events and look for the ways they can produce positive, and equally unexpected, outcomes. If we have a little faith in ourselves. If we persist.

ON CONFIDENCE

Because one believes in oneself, one doesn't try to convince others. Because one is content with oneself, one doesn't need others' approval. Because one accepts oneself, the whole world accepts him or her.

—Lao Tzu

The last thought I want to leave you with is a reflection on the value of confidence. Confidence is one of the most powerful forces we can bring to any endeavor. It is our quiet belief in ourselves, even when we suspect others might not quite believe in us. It's the knowledge that we are intelligent and hardworking and that we can learn what we need to know to make our way in this world. It is the certainty that we are always going to try to do what is right and treat others with respect and that these things matter. Confidence comes from past experiences that have shown all of these things to be true.

We are easily intimidated, all of us. We all have this little goblin that sits on our shoulder constantly causing us to question our decisions, our judgments, and our beliefs. It tells us that we are doing things the wrong way. This goblin likes pointing out how everyone around us is somehow smarter, faster, better, funnier, prettier, kinder, etc. And in a way, the goblin is right. There *is* always someone who is smarter or faster or better or funnier or prettier or kinder.

But the goblin's observation misses the point. There is no one quite like us. In the entire world. The unique combination of our being—our thoughts, our values, our physical appearance, our interior light, our joys, our fears, our beliefs, our soul, and essence—is unique. And this uniqueness, this special, one-of-a-kind person that we each get to be, should be an enormous source of confidence, because we can be the very best "us" we know how. And no one can do that better than we can.

As you embark on the exciting journey before you, I invite you to reach for your confidence in yourself. Remember who you are, where you come from, and what you have accomplished. Know that your family is so very proud of you. Know that there are teachers and coaches and friends who hold you dear. Most of all, know that you are loved wholly, completely, and unconditionally, by your father and me. If you ever find yourself lacking in confidence in yourself, lean on the confidence that we have in you.

We can't wait to see all that you will accomplish in the coming years and to see who you will become. And we can't wait to cheer you on, every step of the way.

Claims of the Flesh

by Kim Nelson

Daughter mine,
You belong to me,
But others claim you.
Going back and back,
All through time,
I can see their arms outstretched,
Yearning for you to do what they could not.

And if you feel their strength
Within you, coursing raw and wild,
Do not be afraid, for these were strong women.
And if their sorrow sometimes saturates you,
Know that they have wept your tears.
And in your moments of ecstatic joy,
Know that they too, have touched the sky,
And celebrate with you.

And when that drumbeat pounds your soul,
Do not fear its wild release.

Let your hips sway to the dance,
It is a part of you.

You may feel that they are watching;
They are.
You may feel them holding you accountable;
They do.

You may feel their love surround you;
It does.

Your life is their legacy.
Their love is your inheritance.
Their expectations are great
And you are ready.

Daughter mine,
You belong to me, but others claim you.
Listen for their whispers in your dreams.
Honor their sacrifice.
Respect their struggle.
All they ever hoped for and dreamed is in you,
And you are ready
To take up this burden.

This above all: to thine own self be true
And it must follow as the night the day,
Thou canst not then be false
Farewell: my blessing season this in thee!

Polonius to Laertes,
Hamlet, Act I, Scene III
William Shakespeare